Faith In the Wait

Everyone has faith.....until they have to have faith

ShaLynn King

Dedication

During a season when I was in constant wait for God. Waiting for Him to heal me, restore me, and everything around me, and receive what He had promised me, this devotional was born. I don't think I waited well, but the fact that I am sitting here says otherwise.

Thank you to everyone who waited with me. Who poured into me when I couldn't even encourage myself. Thank you because it matters who you wait with.

Thank You, God, for the grace You have given me to wait and wait well, seeking You and trusting You. Thank You for entrusting me with this assignment. Allow this devotional to reach who it needs to and change at least 1 person's life, as they too, wait. Allow this to strengthen the reader, encourage them, and keep them seeking You, O Lord, with all their heart, mind, and soul.

Finally, to my husband, I thank Adonai for you.

Introduction

There is something sacred about waiting. Something heavy and quiet and often misunderstood. This devotional was born in that space. In the in between. In the not yet. It is for those who are still holding on even when the promise feels far. For those who are praying and showing up and believing even when it feels like nothing is changing.

Each page carries a reminder that God is near in silence. Through scripture and real stories, you will walk through seasons of trusting, learning, releasing, and growing. These words were written in moments when giving up felt easier, but grace kept showing up. They are here now to walk with you as you wait.

This is not about waiting perfectly. This is about staying close to the One who makes the wait worth it. The One who restores and rewards in His perfect time. As you read, you will be reminded that God is not distant in the delay. He is working. He is shaping. He is preparing you for what He has already prepared for you.

So come as you are. With questions or faith or both. Let these words meet you in your wait. And may they remind you that you are seen. You are held. You are not alone. And this wait is not in vain.

The Grit

"And let us not grow weary in doing good, for in due season we shall reap if we do not lose heart."

Galatians 6:9

Waiting can be hard. But waiting and doing good is even harder. There are many things that cause us to wait and wait well, one being the return of Jesus Christ. While we are waiting, it can be very tempting to get comfortable and return to old habits, mindsets, and language. Being consistent is not always our best strong suit.

Now, yes, there are some people who are able to be consistent with no problem, who have grit. Yet what happens when trials and tribulations come in the midst of everything? It is easy to have a steady routine when your schedule is clear, but what happens when you get married or have a new baby? It is easy to stay faithful to a ministry when everything in your life is going well, but what happens when all hell breaks loose in your life, home, job, and family? How do you show up then? Do not grow weary! I know it can be challenging at times.

And from experience, it can also get boring being consistent in the same area. Just like the Israelites in the wilderness, they were so ready to go back to eating the food from Egypt due to being tired of eating the manna, day in and day out. Yet after 40 years, they finally made it to the promised land. It may take you 40 years to get what you are waiting for, but you will get there. I was listening to a podcast on not jumping ship in your weight loss journey when you stop being motivated and inspired. The speaker said, "You need to stop bailing when things feel boring, because boring is where results are built." * It may be challenging and boring, and hard, but you will get there. So please, do not grow weary in doing good while you wait.

Faith Notes

Waiting With Wings

"But those who wait on the Lord shall renew their strength; they shall mount up with wings like eagles, they shall run and not be weary, they shall walk and not faint."

Isaiah 40:31

This verse has always led me to think and overthink some more. Like, how is this even possible to gain strength in waiting for something? If I am waiting, how will I have the strength to run and not grow tired and walk without fainting? Because chilllee, if you knew me, you would know that running is not my thing, and walking is not a regular part of my routine. So how?

Thank God for His divine wisdom. I had no idea how tiring it is to fight on my own behalf. I had no idea how exhausting it really is to do things in my own strength until God sat me down. No job, just school. I used to be a busybody. One who always had something to do, somewhere to go. I never stayed in the house for more than 24 hours at a time. And to answer your question, how did I make it through the pandemic? I didn't. I was deployed. Life after the Navy, God sat me down for two years, where I was able to work on my bachelor's degree and my master's.

In that is when I learned that waiting on the Lord renews my strength. He was preserving me for what lies ahead. I can't say I was thrilled about it the entire time, but I made it through. I was in my waiting season for so many things, but while I waited, I learned to trust the Lord. To seek Him. To know when to run and when to walk. How far to walk? When it was time to go and when it was time to stop. I waited on Him, so in the waiting, He could renew every ounce of strength I used while doing things on my own.

Faith Notes

Stillness

"Be still, and know that I am God; I will be exalted among the nations, I will be exalted in the earth."

Psalm 46:10

Being still is something that causes so much energy....doesn't it? For someone like me, who again tends to feel the need to be involved in so much, it took so much work to be still. Prior to surrendering my life to Christ, I felt as if things weren't going to get done unless I did it. That people wouldn't get what they needed unless I got myself together. This was a tactic from the enemy to keep me busy and not focused on God.

To keep trusting my own ways other than God's way. To keep me from being still and knowing that God is in control of it all, and He and only He is the I AM of my life. When you are not only still but know who God is, something changes. Something shifts within, especially while you are waiting. Waiting is taunting anyway, we become anxious, fearful of results, our mind starts to wander, often down a rabbit hole, and we do any and everything but be still. I encourage you today to be still and know God. Truly know Him, and then you will see what He is able to do.

Faith Notes

The Work of the Mountain

"So Jesus said to them, 'Because of your unbelief, for assuredly, I say to you, if you have faith as a mustard seed, you will say to this mountain, 'Move from here to there,' and it will move, and nothing will be impossible for you."

Matthew 17:20

In the waiting season, I learned there were so many things within me that needed to be cast out prior to me getting whatever it was I was waiting for. I had unresolved anger and unforgiveness that I thought I had dealt with. It was hidden in the dark places in my heart. It was things I had never thought I would overcome, yet there was residue left. I had to press in and believe that God, the God of Abraham, Issac, and Jacob, would heal me and remove the mountain of unforgiveness from my heart.

Once I realized it, I didn't want to receive anything from the Lord that would compromise what He had promised me. The thing I had been waiting for could have been gone just as quickly as I had gotten it due to my disbelief. I could have ruined a friendship God had for me, a business deal, a job opportunity, a promotion, all due to not waiting and allowing God to do a work in me.

Had I received my husband at a time I was not fully healed, I could have projected my distrust onto him, making a mess of our relationship before it even started. For there is nothing too hard for God, this is true. It is true because He does the impossible, the supernatural, the unthinkable. He is able to do the "hard" thing. The difficult thing. Even the most stubborn mountain is movable if we just have the faith to believe it. Waiting isn't just about the end when we receive it; it's about building faith in God, hope in the Father, and trust in the Trinity. Wait, yet believe He will move whatever He needs to move in order for you to get what is on the other side of the mountain.

Faith Notes

I Want What I Want When I Want It!

"To everything there is a season, a time for every purpose under heaven."

Ecclesiastes 3:1

We often want what we want when we want it. No matter what time it is. Ladies, have you ever had a craving for a specific food or sweet treat in the middle of the night? And nothing could stop you from getting it? I remember I was pregnant with my daughter, and I would often crave slushies. The only problem was that she was born in January. I know a lot of you are saying that it's no problem. Well, we are from up north, where it snows in the winter and gets really cold. Those were the days I wanted the slushy even more. A green apple, please.

Thank goodness the gas station still served the slushies even in the off-season. There are things we often pray for, hoping they will be available to us in the current season we are in, but that is not how God operates. Just sit back and think of all the times you cried out to God asking Him for a job, a spouse, a house, and did not receive it in that season, yet when the time was right, you got it. Maybe it was a promotion or a friendship that you desired. After you receive

12

what you prayed for, in the right time and season, you receive it, isn't it so much better?

Now, remember that time and apply it to this season. You are waiting for God to move. Personally, I am single and waiting for God to bring me my husband. If I got him when I started praying for him 7 years ago, I can tell ya'll now I would be divorced! I was not ready to be anybody's wife! So, thank You, Lord, for not giving me what I wanted in a season it was not ordained for me to have.

Faith Notes

God's Time not Mine

"A little one shall become a thousand, and a small one a strong nation. I, the Lord, will hasten it in its time."

Isaiah 60:22

Time. It has always been my friend, yet not really. I know how could that be? Well, I have always had a way of knowing what time it was without looking at a clock; I would just know. When I started to get in the presence of God and turn to Him, I started to wake up in the morning, on time, with no alarm clock. For me to go from being a hard sleeper and used to having trouble waking up in the mornings, this was a big deal! Yet waiting on God's time was not my strong suit.

I always felt as if I had to rush. I did this in all areas of my life. I was always quick to pass whatever test or skill I needed to advance. I was quick to learn whatever I needed to learn just to get through the test in class or just to pass the class. With that, I did not learn much. Even in my studying, I studied just enough to be prepared for an exam. I walked out with good grades, yet I did not gain anything. With God, in the kingdom, fighting spiritual battles, this is a horrible and lazy tactic.

Thank goodness God knows me better than I know myself. I didn't like going in circles, taking the same test; I felt like a failure.

I felt as if I did not do well the first time. Yet that was not true. God was developing me at that time. With a little here, a little more over here. When it was time for me to receive whatever it was I was searching, seeking, and/or asking for, I was prepared in the time God had for me. I joined the Navy when I was 25. It was an experience, yet at that time, I learned how to live without depending on the help of family and close friends. When it was time for me to be discharged, I moved to a new city where I knew no one. I was prepared. God equipped me for the journey.

In His time, it was beautiful. Had I moved when and where I wanted to, I would have struggled. A few months prior to me seeing a Navy recruiter, I was creating a plan to move to Atlanta with my then 6-year-old daughter. I knew nothing of the city, the school system, and I knew no one. Most importantly, I did not have a real, stable relationship with God.

I went to visit the city and everything! I had a plan to start a couple of businesses, nothing in God's will nor alignment, and I had no clue where we were going to live. Thank God for stopping my plans. What stopped me was my getting laid off from my job at a title company. Putting a damper on my finances, forcing me to join the military to have financial stability and benefits for me and my baby girl. I still moved down south, but not in Atlanta, so for that, I am grateful for the timing of the Lord! Even when we just KNOW we know best.

Faith Notes

_____

_____

_____

_____

_____

_____

_____

_____

_____

_____

_____

_____

_____

_____

Is He First?

"But seek first the kingdom of God and His righteousness, and all these things shall be added to you."

Matthew 6:33

When you make a purchase, what is the first thing you do? Are you the one who checks their bank account first, or are you the one who swipes their card and hopes for the best later? When you wake up in the morning, what is the first thing you do? Check your phone? Scroll social media? Think of all that needs to be done that day? What if, before you gave your brain the chance to think of anything, you hit the floor on your knees and thanked God?

What if, before you left your house, you made any purchases for the day, you stopped and asked God to create a plan for your day? What if you asked Him if this is something He wants you to even buy? How would your life be changed? I remember a time I was struggling financially, but I had a gift card for Sam's Club. I went to the store and shopped, and as I shopped, I was so nervous about going over the amount of what was available because I had nothing extra to give at the time.

As I walked through the store, mentally pricing things and being very cautious of what I was picking up, I heard the Lord tell me, "Get what you want, baby girl". I was a little nervous still, but I got

18

what I needed. Ya'll don't you know I had one cent left on that gift card. I was so in shock that He made sure I was covered. Something similar ended up happening a couple of different times, and each time, I was in awe of the Lord ensuring we had more than enough. Each time, I ended up with more money left over than I intended.

Let me tell you when you seek the Lord first, He will surely make sure you want and need for NOTHING! Prior to walking into Sam's Club, I sought God. While going into any other store, I sought Him, and in seeking Him, He did not let me down. While waiting for the financial breakthrough, seek Him first. While waiting for your family to be redeemed and restored, seek Him first. For He knows everything, He sees everything, He is the beginning and the end. He knew what I was going to purchase before I did, and He knew the total before I even walked into the store, so He guided me, and my role was to trust Him. Seek first His Kingdom! Seek first His Kingdom.

Faith Notes

Keep Knocking, it Works

"Ask and it will be given to you; seek and you will find; knock, and it will be opened to you. For everyone who asks receives, and he who seeks finds, and to him who knocks it will be opened."

Matthew 7:7-8

In March of 2024, I was in Burlington in their journal section, and I came across a journal with this scripture on it. I heard the Lord tell me to get it and use it for prayers for my future husband. I questioned if I had heard Him correctly. It seemed a little silly to use this verse for something I have been praying to God for and waiting on Him for. Not only that, but for my husband! So, as I grabbed it and was walking to the register, God gave me the revelation as to why He chose that one for me. It wasn't until a year later that I received the full revelation of it.

By that time, I was walking in it. I was not consistent in writing in the journal at first. I asked God for a husband, and that was it. Then I started to diligently seek God for my husband. Around that time, God told me He wanted more time with me. I was more at peace with that. When the end of January had come around, God told me to write in that journal daily for three months. That was from February-April, me knocking. I would write prayers based on Scriptures I was led to.

What I didn't know is what God was doing behind closed doors, yet in plain sight. My husband was in the vicinity without my knowledge. I was truly oblivious to this man I would see occasionally. I had no contact with him and didn't even know his name. I had went out with a group of friends and he was there, yet I still knew nothing about him. Even after receiving a word from God who this mystery man was, I was not excused from continuing my assignment in obedience in what God had told me to do, knock, writing in my journal daily.

Ask God. Seek Him. And knock until He answers and you have what you have been asking for.

Faith Notes

Is it Dead or Asleep?

"When He came in, He said to them, "Why make this commotion and weep? The child is not dead, but sleeping."

Mark 5:39

There was a time, while waiting for my husband, that I thought the situation was dead. We met in March, exchanged numbers in April, and by April 30th, we had confirmation that we were to be husband and wife. By the end of that week, we had stopped speaking to one another and I was at loss for words. I felt as if the relationship had died before we even had a chance to come together. During that time, almost two months had passed by, and I just knew I had heard God wrong and he was not my husband, so I gave up. I started to walk away from the situation.

I was set to move on. In that time, I was telling my sister of some things but not all, then God spoke through her, which was in alignment with a dream that I had. Who told me to walk away? Who told me it was dead? I made that decision on my own, out of my own will, own strength, my own knowledge, and revelation from what it had looked like. In that moment when I had given up, while my sister and I sat in my car, we went into worship on the spot.

I had no idea God was going to speak to me then about my husband. I had no idea I was in the wrong and had no right to walk away and label something dead that God said was sleeping. It awakened something in me at that moment. See, sleeping and death look very similar to each other. Only when you get close enough to the person do you see that they are still breathing. Only when you are close enough do you see the truth. When you are close enough to the Lord our Savior, do you see and know if a situation is dead or sleeping? I had trusted what my eyes could see, not what the Lord had said.

There are times when our eyes deceive us. Sometimes we get too invested in the evidence around us and exclude Jesus. It's as if we limit what He can and will do. We have seen Him move in other areas, either in our lives or the lives of others, so when handed a new, or shall I say different or more challenging, situation, we start to doubt He is able to breathe life into it. To make it alive again.

Faith Notes

Confide in the Lord

"And he believed in the Lord, and He accounted it to him for
righteousness."

Genesis 15:6

Believe in the Lord, for it is good. To believe means to "accept (something) as true; feel sure of the truth of". In Hebrew, it means to trust, rely, and confide. When we believe in the Lord, He sees it and honors it. We have free will to believe in whatever we choose, yet there is evidence in what or who we choose to believe in. When we choose to believe the lies of the enemy, it often shows. We become insecure, lack confidence, and react off of assumptions.

Yet when we believe in God, we have confidence, peace, and strength. In this Scripture, we see how Abraham believed in the Lord for His promise to give him descendants and the father of many nations. Although Abraham did not live to see his promise in entirely, God kept His word.

In Galatians 3:6-8, we see evidence of it, for it says, "just as Abraham believed God, and it was accounted to him for righteousness. Therefore, know that only those who are of faith are sons of Abraham. And the Scripture, foreseeing that God would justify the Gentiles by faith, preached the gospel of Abraham beforehand, saying, 'In you all the nations shall be blessed.'" I don't know what you are waiting for. I don't know if it is tangible, some form of healing of a disease or illness.

I don't know if you are waiting for God to save a family member, just know God is a covenant-keeping God. Just as He told Abraham in Genesis, and the story being repeated in Galatians just as God said it would, it will happen.

Faith Notes

Crazy Faith?!?

"Therefore He who supplies the Spirit to you and works miracles among you, does He do it by the works of the law, or by the hearing of faith?"

Galatians 3:5

It is so important to keep your faith in the waiting season, or in general. God doesn't do things because we are under the law, like He did with the Israelites. Read the book of Deuteronomy. All throughout the book, it speaks of the many laws they are to obey and the reward of obeying the law. Today, we are no longer under the covenant of the law, for when Jesus came down in human form to die on the cross, He gave us the gift of eternal life and access to God's grace and mercies, daily.

Now, we are not to abuse His grace but rather grow in it. The more we increase our faith in Him, the more we will experience the many ways of God. We can call on Jehovah Rapha and know He is going to heal us. We worship the God of Abraham, the God of Issac, and the God of Jacob, the covenant-keeping God. The One who speaks a word, and it is so. We know that because of this world He created. Yet it is our faith that allows Him to move and do miracles for us. If you are seeking a miracle, I encourage you to test your faith. Where is it? Is it in the words of man? Are you listening to the counsel of your best friend? Are you trusting what your mama or granny told you years ago? Or are you truly placing your faith, your trust, your hope in the One who is in control of it all?

Faith Notes

Wise Counsel

"That we should no longer be children, tossed to and fro, carried about with every wind doctrine, by the trickery of men, in the cunning craftiness of deceitful plotting."

Ephesians 4:14

In this waiting season, there will be so many voices giving advice, "godly counsel". So many decisions to be made that you are not to make just yet. There will be a time when God may be silent in an area, which will cause you to seek other people if you aren't too careful. In that you will receive more information that will cause you to be tossed to and fro in relation to what God has already spoken to you about. It is wise to be careful about whom you are seeking counsel from.

Yes, you may trust someone, yet the enemy also knows you can trust them. Just as King Ahab was seeking answers in the prophets in 1Kings 22 because he wanted to hear what he wanted to hear, not the truth which the Lord was telling him. He didn't want to hear what the prophet Micaiah had to say, so the Lord put a lying spirit on all the other prophets (v23), so Ahab had no choice but to see Micaiah. So not only will the enemy use your most trusted people, but God will also. He does this so you will seek Him and His word.

Faith Notes

Patience is Key

"I waited patiently for the Lord; and He inclined to me and heard my cry."

Psalm 40:1

Oh, that word patient. How many things or times are we eager to wait for something patiently? Does it depend on the type of day you had? How hungry are you? Maybe it depends on how tired you are. There are times when I can be patient with the people working in fast food because 1. I know my food will be fresh 2. I've developed a sense of compassion since the pandemic due to businesses being short-staffed and 3. I do not want to take any chance of anyone messing with my food.

Most days, I have a sense of peace over me that I truly cannot explain. If I can be completely honest with you, I was not always like this. I would get an attitude when I had to wait. I would often walk away, choose not to wait, or take my frustration out on someone around me. I could not stand waiting! Even today, I do not like traffic, yet there are times I have the patience to sit in it. I don't know if age has any factor in it, but I do believe God had 100% to do with my adjustment. Yet one thing I have yet to grasp is, how is it I can develop a tolerance for traffic but not what my Father has for me?

I mean He knows all, He knows best, He knows me better than I know myself, yet I have trouble waiting on Him. I will say that once I truly surrendered to Yahweh and submitted to the fact that He knows best, I was able to wait patiently on Him. To be honest, what I was waiting for didn't even take as long as I thought it would. I even started to enjoy the waiting season before I received it. At church on Sunday, our Bishop preached, and at the end he said God said, "It will be worth your wait". And that changed everything for me. If God said it is worthwhile, then who am I to be impatient? One thing I know is that God hears us when we cry out to Him. He hears every sob, He hears every question, and every plea. He hears. And He always answers.

Faith Notes

Is It Time to Surrender?

"Your God has commanded your strength; strengthen, O God, what You have done for us. O God, You are more awesome than Your holy places. The God of Israel is He who gives strength and power to His people. Blessed be God."

Psalm 68:28;35

If I can be completely honest with you, I started to lose my faith and hope in God. I know all that He had done for me, but the road was not pretty. As I write this, I am in the middle of waiting to see if God will come through and provide for my child and me financially for our rent before we are evicted. I felt my obedience would have kept me from having any financial difficulties. That my tithes will ALWAYS mean I will never struggle financially. But if I were honest, the last two years have been a strain on my finances.

But year two has been extremely challenging. I trusted that the Lord would always supply my needs... on MY time. I mean, let's be real, His word says that He will..Yet it never says when or how. Due to my not accepting that part of the revelation, I was depleting myself. Not surrendering my strength unto the Lord. I just kept hearing "it's coming", "take one more step", "don't give up", "one more prayer could be the prayer!". It reminded me of the time I was deployed during the pandemic.

We were told we would be returning home in two weeks, and close to the end of the two weeks, we would be told that it would be another two weeks. It was to the point where we weren't told when we would return home. When you are given a date, a timeline, you tend to muster enough strength to make it to that mark. But when it's extended, you gather a little more, yet too many extensions become discouraging. I wonder if this is how infants feel when we try and get them to crawl or walk. We take the toy or whatever it is they want and keep pushing it further away from them to get them to get to it. Oftentimes, we see them sit down or look back, thinking, "Is it worth it?"

Yet as parents, we continue to encourage them. We stand them back up, give them a smile, and tell them, "Come on, you got it!". I believe that is what God does for us, to stretch our faith. For He is our Father, the Creator, the Great I AM. He is Holy. He gives us strength and power to keep going and trample over the serpents as we go. Psalm 24:1 says, "The earth is the Lord's, and all its fullness, the world and those who dwell therein".

He owns it ALL! He knows what to give us and exactly when. Just like He knows the end of my situation. He knows how much strength I need to get through this, when to increase it, along with the amount of power to get me to the other side. All I need to do is trust in Him, surrender unto Him the strength of my flesh and own will.

Faith Notes

Where is your Trust?

"Trust in Him at all times, you people, pour out your heart before Him, God is a refuge for us."

Psalm 62:8

Trust. A word that is not very cute or popular. We often trust without knowing we are trusting in things or people, even places. We take advantage of the fact that certain places will always be around, so we often make plans to visit, then as time goes by, you drive past that place (whether it be a restaurant or store), then it is no longer there. We say we will call someone or text them, yet we become too in tune with our own schedule we get lost in the needs of other people. The only one who is not too busy, never overwhelmed with too much, is God.

He is always available to listen. Not only does the Lord listen to you, He hears you, He understands what you are saying, and all your needs. Oftentimes, when we speak to a friend, spouse, family member, even when we pray to God, we say one thing yet really mean something else, and find ourselves explaining what we said. God knew the first time. Not only does He hear the words coming from your mouth, but He also hears the unspoken words from your heart. He is the safest place to ever be.

Have you ever thought of something in your heart, then boom, it was there? I was thinking one day how I would like a black pair of heels because I had other colors except black. Well, a few weeks later, I went to my mom's house to help her clean, and she had a pair of heels she couldn't fit into because they were too small. She wears a shoe size 11, and I wear a 9! How random was that?! Not random at all, but very strategic. That let me know that God hears even my small request. So, how much more can I trust Him with the larger ones? It may take more trust, faith, and waiting; however, it is not impossible nor unheard of.

Faith Notes

Release the Tears

"My tears have been my food day and night, while they continually say to me, 'Where is your God?'"

Psalm 42:3

How many tears have you cried in your waiting season? How many nights have you cried yourself to sleep? How many tears fell from your eyes after you dropped the kids off at school and before you left school grounds? I know the Scripture says "while THEY continually say to me, 'Where is your God?'", but how many times have YOU said, while crying, where ARE You God? Crying is often necessary.

It is a way to express feelings when no words ever could. When I was younger, I thought crying was a sign of weakness. Yet when we consider infants and children, they often cry as a form of communication when they have no words to express. When your three-year-old child or niece/nephew is sleepy, they often cry or start to whine over any small inconvenience. If we are honest with ourselves, deep down, we would do the same when we are sleepy, too.

When children wake up from a nap, they cry, not because they may need something, they are awakened and do not see their parent or guardian anywhere around them. Yet you are right in the house with them. In another room, sometimes right in front of them, yet their vision is a little distorted, and they didn't quite notice you sitting there. God is right there in front of us; we can't see Him, hear Him, or even feel Him at times, yet He is there. And let's not talk about our enemies asking us where our God is. For if they knew Him in the capacity as we did, they wouldn't dare ask that question, for we KNOW He is all around us.

Isn't it funny how our attitude switches and the answer changes when it's an outsider questioning our God and His whereabouts? It is so easy to stand up and voice where our Father is when we are being taunted by someone else, yet when we get in our room behind closed doors, we ask Him, the One who is all around us, Where are You? I advise you, next time you are in tears, in the middle of a storm, a wait, whatever it is, and instead of questioning God's location, simply say "thank You for being here".

Faith Notes

Embrace the Wait

"I know that You can do everything, and that no purpose of Yours can be withheld from You."

Job 42:2

Sometimes knowing God can do everything is the exact reason why we struggle in the wait. Because God, at any moment You can release whatever I need, the very thing I'm seeking You for, place it right into my hands and still be amazing and great. If He did that every time, would the praise, worship, glory, and honor we give Him be just as great each time? Would our worship and revelation of Him become greater? God is very intentional and purposeful in all that He does.

Once we come to the revelation of this, it releases the pressure we feel in the wait. I just got a revelation that I will never get this season back. The season of me being single, living in an apartment as a single mother. I will never be in this financial bind again. The praise and worship I have will not be like this ever again. I say that because when God does all that I have been waiting for, my worship will shift. It will be deeper, greater, different. I will have experienced God in a new way, so no way I can praise and worship Him on that level. While I am typing this, I have no clue how the story will end for me. How He will bring my future husband, if I will be evicted from my apartment, or if I will be able to get pregnant in the future due to being diagnosed with PCOS. But I do know God is purposeful in ALL that He does. I do know Elohim is able to do everything.

Faith Notes

Pen & Paper

"Then the Lord answered me and said: 'Write the vision and make it plain on tablets, that he may run who reads it. For the vision is yet for an appointed time; but at the end it will speak, and it will not lie. Though it tarries, wait for it; because it will surely come, it will not tarry."

Habakkuk 2:2-3

Writing has become a form of release to me. Writing about how I feel, what I think, and what I experience. There is something about an old-fashioned pen and paper session between God and me. He is the only One who can see it and is able to read it. I have written so many visions of what I wanted my husband to look like. What car I would love to drive, what house I wanted to live in. As I grew in the Lord, some things changed. Some attributes stayed the same.

The more I delighted myself in the Lord, the more my desires shifted to His, giving me the right vision to write. Not everything will come in a snap of our fingers, yet if a true vision is from the Lord, it will happen. It shall come to pass. God is not a man that He shall lie. He gives no false vision. Yet it is something about being able to go back to that piece of paper from a notebook or binder and seeing exactly what you wrote come into fruition. To write the vision in one state, in a season where nothing makes sense, then to see it and look back and see the journey it took to get there, is another level of glory.

I don't know if you are like me, but there are times when I forget about a vision or something I wrote. But the Lord will always bring me back to it, and all I can say is "wow". Like God really was the One with the pen in His hand. He really was preparing me for what was to come. This is the true definition of our thoughts not being our own. God truly knows all! It's like He is revealing a secret in what He is going to do in our lives by giving us a "thought" to write down. No vision will be wasted. Not one.

Faith Notes

What's the Goal? Press!

"Not that I have already attained, or am already perfected; but I press on, that I may lay hold of that for which Christ Jesus has already laid hold of me"

Philippians 3:12

Today was a fresh day for me. I went to church, and our Bishop preached on fatigued faith. If this wasn't what I needed to hear! Listen, it is okay to be tired. It is quite alright to feel fatigued in your faith as if you are about to give up. Even if you tell God you want to give up, He is okay with that as well. Waiting is hard! Believing in something that seems impossible is very hard! Even the story in the Bible where the father is speaking to Jesus about healing his son asked Jesus, the HEALER, to help his unbelief! Who are we not to do the same? Who are we to feel we have it all together?

The people in the Bible didn't have the Bible to reference. They had to live their life in full and complete total trust and in faith. They didn't know what Jesus would look like, yet when some saw Him, they knew who He was. They had no guidance on the voice they were hearing was of the Lord. Sammuel is the only one mentioned in the Bible who had someone teach him how to discern the voice of the Lord. Even Eli missed it the first two times.

We are in challenging times with additional sources that were not available back in those times (i.e., social media), and yet they pressed through. Paul tells us to press on in this verse. We shall, we must, keep pressing on because we are not whole and complete in Christ just yet. There are things that need to be learned at this time. This is a season you may never encounter again. You may miss something about the wait once you come out of it. Just whatever you do, don't settle here, press on.

Faith Notes

Being Content is not Settling

"Not that I speak in regard to need, for I have learned in whatever state I am, to be content."

Philippians 4:11

We all have a need or want for something. If we are honest with ourselves, we at times tend to desire more. More money. More house. More friends. More food. More of anything except responsibility. It's as if the things we have are not enough for us. That what God has provided for us isn't good enough. Is being content too difficult for us? Is the mere fact that we have all we need in this season displeasing to us?

I know we are talking about waiting, yet in the wait, if we become more content in the state we are in, the wait becomes shorter. There was a point where I had to be real with myself that if it is never God's will that I marry, will I be content? It is easier for me to be content with not having more children than it is that I will spend the rest of my nights alone. Is it easier for you to be content when it's less compromising? For the woman with no children, is it easier to be content in having a career where you travel than it is for you to be childless? Or the woman who has a full-time job, is it easier to be content in knowing you have a stable job rather than starting the hair salon business God called you to?

It is easy for us to be content with what is comfortable. This is not the contentment Paul is speaking of. It is being content even if we do not receive the very thing we are desiring God to do. Just like Shadrach, Meshach, and Abed-Nego, they told King Nebuchadnezzar that even if God didn't deliver them from the fiery furnace, they would not bow down to his god. They were in expectation, full of faith, that God would deliver them, yet if He didn't, they did not change their position about serving the Lord God Almighty. I ask you, what area are you not content with? Check in with yourself. Ask God to come in and show you where you need to surrender it to Him to be more content.

Faith Notes

Embrace the Comforter

"Blessed be the God and Father of our Lord Jesus Christ, the Father of mercies and God of all comfort, who comforts us in all our tribulation, that we may be able to comfort those who are in any trouble, with the comfort with which we ourselves are comforted by God."

2 Corinthians 1:3-4

During this time, I had God comforted me. I had the hands of the Holy Spirit guiding me, giving me everything I needed each and every day. If it had not been for the Lord, I truly would have lost my mind. God didn't take me through this just for me. He didn't have me write this devotional just to continue to review it every time I feel down or need a reminder. He brought me through so I may be a comforter to others. I may not be able to sit next to you, speak directly to your situation, or hug you and tell you that everything will be alright.

What I can do is lift you, the reader, up in a prayer that every time you pick up this book that you feel the warmth of the Holy Spirit just as I did while going through the tribulations of waiting. I pray that you not only come through to the other side, but you come through stronger, wiser, full of more power from the Holy Spirit, and able to comfort the next person you see going through a waiting season. A season when it is getting harder to trust God.

Rather, it is a move to a new city, country, or town, leaving everything and everyone you know behind for the sake of the Lord. Or maybe you are waiting for a report from the doctor after God declared you healed, and you are ensuring the lab results will testify. Maybe you are waiting for your future husband, a family member, to be saved and return to the Lord. Whatever it is, I ask You Lord to comfort Your child. Wrap them in Your arms, let them feel Your presence in a mighty way. Embrace them like You've never done before.

Even if they are reading this for the fifth time, embrace them deeper than the last four times. Comfort and strengthen your children. Love them. Meet them where they are, God, amen.

Faith Notes

He is Abel

"Yes, we had the sentence of death in ourselves, that we should not trust ourselves but in God who raises the dead."

2 Corinthians 1:9

God raised the dead! Did you read that?! He did it with no help. There were no prayers needed. He spoke, and Jesus rose from the grave. Now I don't know about you, but that is the God I serve! I serve a mighty God. If He is able to do that, how much more is He able to do? How much more can He do without involving man? I wish I'd known what your situation is today, but better yet, God does. He knows all and hears all. He sees what we can't and knows what we do not.

Even when we think we have a need in one area, He knows about the needs in the other areas as well. He is truly trustworthy. Our God is perfect. Even the pain we have experienced, He had a purpose for that, whether we gained revelation of it or not, just yet. Even if it was to simply give Him glory for bringing you out, Yahweh is still good. We should still place our trust in Him. Trust Him, for He is good. Our Creator is so good, He needs no help proving He is good.

Do you know anyone who can create something just by speaking? I sure don't. Is there anyone whom you know of that you can fully trust, who is perfect in every area in every way? I certainly do not. There are times when I question why people even trust me. Can I be trusted in some ways? Of course I can. However, I would not trust myself, or anyone else, because we are all flawed. Yahweh is the only perfect one who is capable to do what we are incapable of doing. He needs no assistance, so why not place all your trust in Him? Trust in the One who is able to raise the dead.

Faith Notes

Stay the Course

"That good thing which was committed to you, keep by the Holy Spirit who dwells in us."

2 Timothy 1:14

That good thing is the thing God spoke over you years, months, weeks, days, even hours ago. It doesn't matter when it was spoken; it was spoken. The word committed means: feeling dedication and loyalty to a cause, activity, or job; wholeheartedly dedicated. Now, if you really know God, then you know He does nothing half-heartedly. He does nothing partially, yet everything in its entirety. He is wholeheartedly seeking us, protecting us, healing us, restoring us. He does it and does it all well.

Jesus didn't partially die on the cross for a portion of our sins; no, He died for all of our sins. He is so committed to the good thing that He is watching it all the way through. When you receive the prophetic word, give it to the Holy Spirit to guard, nurture, and protect, that it may grow. That there is no room for the enemy to take it, delay it, or hinder it from coming to pass. Allow the Holy Spirit to keep it so that when you are growing weary or even when you have forgotten, it is within you.

Faith Notes

Win Win

"The charge I commit to you, son Timothy, according to the prophecies previously made concerning you, that by them you may wage the good warfare having faith and good conscience, which some having rejected concerning the faith have suffered shipwreck."

1 Timothy 1:18-19

We have a choice to either embrace the prophecies spoken over us or reject them. There is a difference between warfare and shipwreck. In wars, there are usually a winning side and a losing side. In a shipwreck, there is catastrophe, death, and chaos. Warfare may feel like there is chaos going around, yet that is the thing, it FEELS like it is.

By now, we all know that we should not, cannot trust our feelings. But in the shipwreck, there usually is no turning back, no restoration, and as the text reads, it is suffering. When Paul speaks about warfare, he says to "wage the good warfare," which means to carry on. To carry on the good warfare of the faith. While waiting and believing for promises to come to pass, there will be warfare that we must carry through to get to the promise. Sadly, not everyone makes it to their promise.

They give up, reject it, step out of alignment with God and His plan for them because the warfare becomes too heavy. This is true, or else Paul wouldn't have said it. We all "struggle" with something, especially when we are waiting, in lack, or lonely. Yet choose to wage the good warfare of the faith in the Lord. That is the only way to get through, in the strength of the Lord. Call on Him. Depend on Him. Worship Him through it. He is there with open arms.

Faith Notes

_____

_____

_____

_____

_____

_____

_____

_____

_____

_____

_____

_____

You are not Forgotten

"I will say to God my Rock, 'Why have You forgotten me? Why do I go mourning because of the oppression of the enemy?"

Psalm 42:9

There have been so many times I have felt forgotten by God. So many times I felt as if the words He had spoken over me were going to happen so far into the future, or He had "accidentally" given my blessing to someone else. That I was not going to get mine now because He had somehow ran out. Or second-guessed that the blessing or thing I was told was for me was actually for someone else. Silly right? Yet how many of us have actually felt like this at some time in our lives?

Honestly! I kept hearing that I was not forgotten about, that God did not forget about me. Yet the evidence was so loud! It was the complete opposite if you had asked me. I had gotten to the point where I just settled that it would not happen for me, or it was never for me to begin with. I felt as if those around me were more blessed than I. I wasn't doing enough to receive anything from God. Yet I know God is my Rock. He is my firm foundation. Rocks are solid. They can handle any type of weight, and if thrown, they can cause damage to property. God is my Rock! It amazes me how we can stand on something that is firm and yet still feel as if it has forsaken or forgotten us.

It's not that we forget we walk on foundations every day, such as the ground, sidewalks, and building structures, we get so used to it being there and we trust in it so much so we often do not think twice when we step on them. How is it we trust in that more than our God? Our Lord and Savior, who created the grounds we walk on? Yahweh is more solid than the structure of the ground. David poses a good question: why do we go mourning? Why? For God is not an unjust God. He has no favorites. He is just and righteous in all His ways. And from one girl who felt God had forgotten her, He surely has not forgotten you.

Faith Notes

The Middle...

"Why are you cast down, O my soul? And why are you disquieted within me? Hope in God; for I shall yet praise Him, the help of my countenance and my God."

Psalm 42:11

As women, our feelings and emotions can feel as if they are all over the place at times. We may not know how to feel or how we went from feeling on top of the world, filled with so much joy and love. Then, not even a full 24 hours later, we feel depleted, lack motivation, and even love. We feel forgotten about, we feel forsaken, we feel as if we aren't good enough. In those times, it may even seem as if nothing will even help. We will stay in that pit, in that dark place, for a while, especially in the middle of the wait.

The thing about the middle is, there really is no way of telling how close you are to the promise or the start. There is a part of the "middle" that isn't really the middle anymore. It is the part where we are almost there, yet not quite there. In this place, is when our soul feels cast down, we are sad, just about to give up hope. The secret key to getting through and withstanding this portion of the wait is to praise. That is one thing the enemy truly cannot take. If you don't feel like singing, you can dance, if no dancing, clap, if no clapping, tap, no tapping, tap your toes, if not that you can say thank you, Lord. Or you can write it.

Nothing can stop your praise! Nothing! So make it a point today to praise Him. Praise Him in whatever form or fashion you can today. Even if you just play a song and sit in the presence of God.

Faith Notes

Trust the Word in the Process

"So shall My word be that goes forth from My mouth; it shall not return to Me void, but it shall accomplish what I please, and it shall prosper in the thing for which I sent it."

Isaiah 55:11

God is faithful in what He does and speaks. He is able to do all that He speaks of. Just look at the many stories and testimonies in the Bible. Look at your life and the things He has already brought you through. If He said it, it will happen. Abraham did not live long enough to see the promise of God come to pass, yet God still made him the father of many nations as He told him when Abraham was 85 years old.

Age does not limit God. Numbers do not intimidate God! If He told you He will provide for you, and your income is $5,000 a month and your bills are $8,000 a month, He will provide. If He told you to write the book, start the business, move to a new city, state, or country, and you only have -$250 in your account, and He told you He will supply all your needs, Jehovah Jireh will supply ALL your needs. Yahweh is not man, He will not trick us into believing something that is not true just to laugh at us as we struggle. He is not a liar! My word says that satan is the father of lies, so if that title is taken, and not by the Almighty God, then what does that say about our Lord and Savior? That He can not and will not lie.

Because He is Alpha and Omega, He knows the end, that is why His word will not come back to Him void. It will accomplish what He says it will. Whose report will you believe? I believe the report of the Lord! That everything He spoke, and still speaking over me, will speak over me in time to come, will happen. It will come to pass, it has no choice but to because my God is no liar.

Faith Notes

The Promise

"For all the promises of God in Him are Yes, and in Him Amen to the glory of God through us."

2 Corinthians 1:20

Let us all touch and agree right now. I may not know you, will never meet you, I have no clue what your situation is or what you are waiting and trusting God to do, but I know the word and all God's promises are yes and Amen, so I say yes and Amen with you. I believe God is going to do mighty things for you. I will not put a time stamp on it because only God can do that, for He is the Author and Creator of time.

Yet read carefully that verse, it says "all the promises of God IN Him" in Him. That does not apply to just any ole thing. It does not apply to what you are hoping God to do that He did not promise you because it does not align with His will, it says the promises IN Him. Only you know the promises that were made in Him; there is also a whole book with 66 other books within it that is filled with promises from God. When you are in alignment with God, all of them belong to you. Every last promise is yours. So we say yes and amen!

Faith Notes

Hope

"Remember the word to Your servant, upon which You have caused me to hope"

Psalm 119:49

In the last stretch of waiting, we often start to become a little disappointed that it hasn't come to pass as of yet. We start to get frustrated with God. What if God told you something, something you hadn't even prayed for, He said He would give you. Had God not told you that, you wouldn't have even hoped for it in the first place. David felt the same way. God, You told me I was going to be married, and I am still single. You told me we were going to have a baby, and I have yet to be pregnant, or I can't seem to carry any baby full term.

God, You said you would bless us financially, yet more bills are piling up, and our income just decreased. I would have never hoped for this had You not spoken this! That is real, raw emotions. Return God's words back to Him. Remind Him of the promises He made you. There is no harm in that. David is one of my favorite people in the Bible because he did so many great things, yet we often look over his realness, authenticity. David danced, undignifiedly, in front of all those people, and even his wife was embarrassed. David prayed prayers against his enemies that aren't usually preached in church. David was real! David shows us, it is ok to be human, have feelings, and cry out to God with them.

"God, I'm tired of waiting, when? just when will You do it for me? I see You doing it for others. When will it be my turn? God, I didn't even want this, yet You said I will have it." As I sit here, I am reminded of the Shunammite woman who didn't ask Elisha the prophet for a son, yet God said He would grant her one, and the son died. Through Elisha, God raised the boy from the dead, yet she wouldn't have been in this situation had God not spoken it and given her a child. Something she lacked and did not request. God, we thank You for the word, yet remember us. Remember Your word spoken over us. Because of Your word, we have hope and Hope in You.

Faith Notes

It's Time

"You shall arise and have mercy on Zion; for the time to favor her, yes, the set time, has come"

Psalm 102:1

There is definitely a time for favor. Where everything that you touch, walk through, and do will be favored by God. I believe that takes place within the waiting season for some, for a reason. To boost our hope and faith in the Lord. To remind us it isn't over and He hasn't forgotten us. It's often a gateway to the promise. Now, when I speak on this, yes, favor follows us all the days of our lives, yet there comes a time when we sometimes don't feel favored by God. Let's be real here. I believe God limits our favor for a season to keep it for when we really need it.

When we have waited for so long, and things around us are just getting worse, and it looks like the complete opposite of what God said. Let the favor of God be upon you today oh daughter of Zion. Let it pour out like rain. May you walk, dwell, and rest in the favor of the Lord, for He has not forgotten you; He is with you.

Faith Notes

www.ingramcontent.com/pod-product-compliance
Lightning Source LLC
Chambersburg PA
CBHW070349130626
46556CB00007B/3094